THE POWER TO BLESS

BOB RODGERS

ISBN: 1-931600-05-8

THE POWER TO BLESS

Published by:
Bob Rodgers Ministries
P.O. Box 19229
Louisville, KY 40259

THE POWER TO BLESS

TABLE OF CONTENTS

THE POWER TO BLESS

CHAPTER 1
THE MEANING OF BLESSINGS

"Blessed be the God and Father of our Lord Jesus Christ, who hath blessed us with all spiritual blessings in heavenly places in Christ."
--Ephesians 1:3

"Blessed be the God and Father of our Lord Jesus Christ, who has blessed us with every spiritual blessing in the heavenly places in Christ."
--Hebrews 6:14

Of all the creations that God made, we are the only ones that can talk. Every word that God spoke to man was a word of blessing. Our words can either bless or curse people.

A few months ago, while I was "Prayer Walking" around the city of Louisville, I saw some men cutting firewood. I said to them, *"God bless you!"* They said, *"Thank you."* Then I said, *"May you make a lot of money today."* Later, they went to get some coffee in a store. A man bought $500 worth of firewood. The fellow told his wife, *"A preacher came by and blessed me and said, 'May you make a lot of money.' "* He made more money cutting firewood that day, than ever before. His wife and father began to come to the church. It is the power to bless, and the power to curse.

This book can literally change your life. You can bless your family. You can bless your employer. You can bless your church. You can bless yourself.

All this is possible, if you understand the principles of THE POWER TO BLESS!

There are five meanings of a blessing:

1. To make whole, by spoken words. Jesus said, "Wilt thou be made whole?" Then He spoke the word of healing; and the person was healed from blindness.
2. To ask and invoke God's divine favor. "God, will you bless me? God, will you help me?"
3. To wish a person well. "Be blessed!"
4. To make happy and prosperous. "I've been blessed by God and His bountiful blessings."
5. To gladden, to glorify or praise. "I bless this person; he has done a terrific job."

> *"And I will make of thee a great nation, and I will bless thee, and make thy name great; and thou shalt be a blessing: And I will bless them that bless thee, and curse him that curseth thee: and in thee shall all families of the earth be blessed."*
>
> *--Genesis 12:2-3*

These fifty words made a difference in the history of the world. The fact is, these words are still in effect today. I am blessed because of this blessing that God spoke.

Not everyone understands the meaning of a blessing. I really believe that many people talk about

God's blessings, but do not even understand the power of **"God bless you."** A blessing is not to be taken for granted. The words that we speak either bless people or they bring a curse to people. Our words bless us, or curse us.

We must understand that there is power in the words that we speak. The world often speaks like, **"Go to hell."** They quickly use the word "hell" in their vocabulary. If they really knew the meaning of hell, I do not think they would do that.

A number of years ago, my wife and I were on an island. We went to where a volcano was. They had ropes keeping people back. I climbed over the rope and I went to get a better look at the volcano. As I was looking down right into the fire pit, I could see the brimstone. I really believe this is what hell is like. I believe when there is an eruption of a volcano, it is hell enlarging itself.

If people only knew the power of hell. You would not want your worst enemy to go there. You do not want anybody to go to that terrible place.

God wants you to BE a Blessing: and to BE BLESSED!

SPEAK POSITIVE BLESSINGS TO OTHERS

There was a manager of a minor league baseball team. He jerked the centerfielder because of an error. And then ran on the field himself showing him how one should play center field. The next batter hit one and a bad bounce hit this manager in the mouth. Then another hit came and he lost it in the sun, and it hit him in the head. Then there was a long line drive that hit him in the eye. The manager was so furious he ran back into the dugout and shook the center fielder and shouted, "You've got center field so messed up, even I can't do a thing with it!"

We need to learn to speak positive blessings to others, instead of negative words.

THE POWER TO BLESS

CHAPTER 2

BINDING AND LOOSING: IMPARTING THE BLESSING

> *"Verily I say unto you, Whatsoever ye shall bind on earth shall be bound in heaven: and whatsoever ye shall loose on earth shall be loosed in heaven. Again I say unto you, That if two of you shall agree on earth as touching any thing that they shall ask, it shall be done for them of my Father which is in heaven."*
>
> *--Matthew 18:18-19*

I want to share with you about an impartation of a blessing. Not many people understand what it means when someone shakes your hand and says, *"God bless you."* We take it so lightly. Sometimes there is no meaning behind it. We just use it as, *"How are you doing?"*, when we really do not care how they are doing. *"Wonderful weather out there, isn't it?"* We use that as small talk. Sometimes we use "God bless you" like small talk. But there is great power and great significance when you say to someone, *"God bless you!"*

You are loosing the power of heaven upon someone. You are declaring, *"Thy will on earth as it is in heaven."* In heaven, there is no sickness. In heaven, there is no poverty. In heaven, all of your needs are met. So when you say, *"God bless you"* you are speaking peace and life to your fellow man.

The Bible says, *"Whatsoever we bind on earth, is bound in heaven. Whatsoever we loose on earth, is loosed in heaven."*

What is a blessing?

What does it mean to be blessed?

A blessing is simply an impartation of God's mercy, God's favor, and God's gifts. That is what a blessing is. When you stand and you begin to bless, you begin to impart God's grace and God's mercy. There is a marked difference.

> *"And I will give unto thee the keys of the kingdom of heaven: and whatsoever thou shalt bind on earth shall be bound in heaven: and whatsoever thou shalt loose on earth shall be loosed in heaven."*
> *--Matthew 16:19*

We have power to bind and loose. If the principles within this book really get a hold of your life, it can change your destiny. It can change where you will be this time next year. It can change and influence your grandchildren.

Again, what is the main principle?

God has called us to bless and not to curse!

I am not just talking about you getting blessed. That is important. We need to be blessed. The blessings of

God are not an option. In the Book of Deuteronomy, God commanded these blessings to come upon us, because if the blessings did not come upon the people, and they did not multiply and increase, they could not take the Promised Land. They had to be blessed, in order for them to conquer the enemy.

> *"But thou shalt remember the LORD thy God: for it is he that giveth thee power to get wealth, that he may establish his covenant which he sware unto thy fathers, as it is this day."*
> *--Deuteronomy 8:18*

Today, we live in a time where it seems like the church does not bless. But God showed me that if we will begin to proclaim and release, and impart life to the blessings of God, we are going to see a mighty wave of blessings come upon our lives, our family, our children and we literally will not be able to contain what God is getting ready to do.

But there has to be an impartation. The impartation has to come from you. It has to come from your lips. You've got to begin to bless your job and bless your money. You've got to begin to speak greatness into your family. Be known as a person who blesses and not a person of destruction. That is what I want to be known as. I want to be a blesser. I want to be someone that imparts blessings, and not curses.

> *"Bless them which persecute you: bless, and curse not. Rejoice with them that do rejoice, and weep with them that weep. Be of the same mind one toward another. Mind not high things, but condescend to men of low estate. Be not wise*

in your own conceits. Recompense to no man evil for evil. Provide things honest in the sight of all men. If it be possible, as much as lieth in you, live peaceably with all men. Dearly beloved, avenge not yourselves, but rather give place unto wrath: for it is written, Vengeance is mine; I will repay, saith the Lord. Therefore if thine enemy hunger, feed him; if he thirst, give him drink: for in so doing thou shalt heap coals of fire on his head. Be not overcome of evil, but overcome evil with good."

--Romans 12:14-21

It says we are to bless, and not to curse. Get the context with which this was written in. This was written in a time when Christians were being persecuted. Christians had curses on them. They were beheaded or fed to the lions. They were dragged off and killed, or were tortured to death. Yet Paul said to bless and not curse.

NEW YORK CITY'S MAYOR LA GUARDIA

Mayor LaGuardia of New York City was one of the most famous mayors of that great city. One evening he went to one of the poorest districts in that city. He dismissed the judge and said, "Tonight, I am going to be the judge."

A lady was brought before him who had stolen a loaf of bread from a storekeeper. He asked the lady, "Why did you steal the loaf of bread?" Her reply, "I didn't have anything to eat. Neither did my daughter, nor my grand-daughter that is living with me."

He looked at the storekeeper, "You're not going to prosecute her over that are you?" He said, "I sure am! We have to make her an example or others will steal from us."

LaGuardia fined her ten dollars and took ten dollars out of his own billfold to pay the fine. He said, "I also fine every person in this court room 50 cents for living in a city where people have to steal to eat." He took his hat and passed it around the courtroom and gave all the money to the lady.

THE POWER TO BLESS

CHAPTER 3

BLOOD LINE COVENANT BLESSINGS IN THE BIBLE

"When the Day of Pentecost had fully come, they were all with one accord in one place. And suddenly there came a sound from heaven, as of a rushing mighty wind, and it filled the whole house where they were sitting. Then there appeared to them divided tongues, as of fire, and one sat upon each of them. And they were all filled with the Holy Spirit and began to speak with other tongues, as the Spirit gave them utterance."

--Acts 2:1-4

The Word of God teaches in the Book of Acts that *"They were in all one accord in one place, and the Holy Spirit fell."* There were flaming torches of fire that sat upon the people. There was a wind that began to sound like an airplane taking off. Then the people began to speak in other tongues as the Spirit gave them utterance or the words to speak. The sign of the New Covenant to the Church was on the people's mouths.

In the Old Testament, the sign came through the act of circumcision. That meant the Covenant was passed on through the bloodlines. You were blessed if you were a descendent of Abraham.

But in the New Covenant, it came upon the tongue.

The Bible says, "They spoke with other tongues." It was a sign that now the blessing was not in the bloodline, but it was whosoever could hear and receive the promise by faith, they could receive the blessing. "He who hath an ear to hear, let him hear what the Spirit saith unto the churches."

We believe in the power of speaking blessings. We believe that whatsoever we bind on earth is bound in heaven. We can bind the devil. We can also loose those that are held captives by the enemy, and they shall be set free.

God commanded the priest to stand before the congregation and bless the people.

God spoke to me, almost four years ago, *"I want you to begin to bless the people."* Every Sunday I would begin to pronounce blessing upon the church, *"May you succeed when others fail. May God's blessing come upon you and overtake you. Your children shall succeed for the glory of God. No weapon formed against you shall prosper."*

Every week I would speak blessings to them physically, spiritually and financially.

God spoke to the priest and said, *"I want you to bless the people."* They would stand and stretch their hands and declare, *"The Lord bless thee and keep thee. The Lord make His face to shine upon thee, and be gracious upon thee. The Lord lift his countenance upon thee; and give thee peace."*

This is not just an Old Testament principle. This is a today principle. Where in the Bible does it say we are to stop blessing. We are never to stop releasing blessings to people. Who gave anyone the authority to stand and say, "Those days are over?" Those days are not over! The New Testament proclaims that we are priests and priestesses forever, after the order of Melchizedek.

> *"Thou art a priest for ever after the order of Melchizedek."*
>
> *--Hebrews 7:17*

Melchizedek blessed Abraham and laid his hands upon him. Abraham brought an offering unto Melchizedek and paid tithes. Now the Bible proclaims that the greater has to bless the lesser. Melchizedek is a picture of Jesus. He has no beginning of days. He has no genealogies. Where did he come from? He was the priest of Jerusalem. This is the city of the most-high God. It is a picture of the New Jerusalem.

Yet Abraham was the father of faith. Out of his seed came Isaac. Out of Isaac's seed came Jacob. Then came the 12 patriarchs, including Levy. From his seed, came Moses and Aaron and the priesthood. If you were a member of the priesthood, you had to be able to quote your genealogy. If they could not prove their genealogy, they could not be a priest. Now comes the word of the Lord. You are not a priest after the order of Aaron, because someone greater than Aaron is here. You have been elevated to the order of Melchizedek.

> *"But ye are a chosen generation, a royal priesthood, an holy nation, a peculiar people; that ye should show forth the praises of him who hath called you out of darkness into his marvelous light:"*
>
> *--I Peter 2:9*

Our mission as priests and priestesses is to bless. God did not call us to curse. But we have the right and the mission and the authority and the responsibility to bless!

Someone said, *"Brother Bob, I do not know how to bless. I do not know how to release a prophetic blessing upon someone. Don't you have to be a prophet? Don't you have to be a preacher?"*

No. You have to be a Believer. You have to believe the Word of God.

> *"And the woman bare a son, and called his name Samson: and the child grew, and the LORD blessed him."*
>   *--Judges 13:24*

God blessed this boy. The Word of God does not say that He blessed other children. I am sure He did. But Samson was blessed. Samson made a difference because he was blessed. When the Spirit of God would come upon Samson, he was not like any other child in the whole nation of Israel that ever was before, or has been since. God's strength came upon him. It was the strength of a superman.

When we think of Samson, we think of a fellow who is probably built like Mr. Universe with big muscles. On no! If he had been a man of mighty muscles they would have known where his strength came from. They had no idea where his strength came from. But it came from God. And the reason it did, is because God blessed him.

SIR ROBERT WATSON WATT

The fellow who invented radar was Sir Robert Watson Watt. One day he was arrested in Canada for speeding in a radar trap. He invented the radar trap. He wrote a poem after he received the ticket:

> *"Pity Sir Robert Watson Watt,*
> *strange target of his radar plot.*
> *And this, with others, I could mention,*
> *A victim of his own invention."*

WHAT IS A BLESSING?

We read the story of Joseph.

> *"And the LORD was with Joseph, and he was a prosperous man; and he was in the house of his master the Egyptian. And his master saw that the LORD was with him, and that the LORD made all that he did to prosper in his hand. And Joseph found grace in his sight, and he served him: and he made him overseer over his house, and all that he had he put into his hand."*
>
> *--Genesis 39:2-4*

That is what the blessing will do. The blessing will come upon you and you may not have anything. But if you will listen and be faithful to God, God will promote you. Joseph became one of the wealthiest men in the world. He saved his family from being destroyed during a worldwide famine.

The Bible talks about the priest in the Book of Numbers. God commanded Aaron and his sons pronounce the blessing. They would stand before the congregation, *"May the Lord bless thee, and keep thee. The Lord make His face to shine upon thee, and be gracious unto thee. Tbe Lord lift up His countenance upon thee, and give you peace!"*

--Numbers 6:24-26

We are in the priesthood, too. We are a royal priesthood. We are a chosen generation. God has commanded us to BLESS! So we stand and we bless the people we work for. We bless our enemies. We bless situations that are hopeless and situations that have no answer to them. We stand and we bless it in the Name of the Lord.

JOB IN THE OLD TESTAMENT

God wants YOU to impart blessing?

Let's look at the Book of Job. We know the story of Job. He was the wealthiest man in the world. However, he soon lost it all---his family, his wealth, even his wife became angry with him. She said to him, *"Why don't you just curse God and die?!"* Then when he rebuked his wife, she got mad at him and she turned to him and said, *"You've even got bad breath."(Job 19:7)* Then his friends condemned him, *"Job, you have sin in your life."*

One of his friends spoke the following words in an effort to encourage him.

"Acquaint now thyself with him, and be at peace: thereby good shall come unto thee. Receive, I pray thee, the law from his mouth, and lay up his words in thine heart. If thou return to the

Almighty, thou shalt be built up, thou shalt put away iniquity far from thy tabernacles. Then shalt thou lay up gold as dust, and the gold of Ophir as the stones of the brooks. Yea, the Almighty shall be thy defense, and thou shalt have plenty of silver. For then shalt thou have thy delight in the Almighty, and shalt lift up thy face unto God. Thou shalt make thy prayer unto him, and he shall hear thee, and thou shalt pay thy vows. Thou shalt also decree a thing, and it shall be established unto thee: and the light shall shine upon thy ways."

--Job 22:21-28

Begin to decree a thing. Command it to come forth. Speak it out. Decree it! *"You shall have gold as dust; and plenty of silver."*

Have you blessed yourself today? Or have you cursed yourself today?

"This is more than I can handle. I just give up. I will never get ahead in life. These bills are about to destroy me. I am going to have a nervous breakdown."

Did you know you are cursing yourself?

But the Bible says we have the power to bless!

"Whatsoever we bind on earth, shall be bound in heaven. Whatever we loose on earth, shall be loosed in heaven."

--Matthew 16:19

What happened to Job?

Job began to decree blessings. He started blessing his money, his wife, and his friends. That's right, his friends were cursing him. Was he cursing them back? He probably felt like it. But he began to pray for them.

> *"And the LORD restored Job's losses when he prayed for his friends. Indeed the LORD gave Job twice as much as he had before."*
> *--Job 42:10*

The Lord gave him twice as much as he had before! How did he get twice as much? The man did not have any money. He was broke; he lost everything. God sent him friends and *"every man gave him a piece of money." (Job 42:11)* His friends came and gave him an offering. They gave him gold. He took that gold and he began to speak to it. *"Gold, you are going to prosper for me. Gold, you are going to make me rich. Gold, you are going to multiply."*

He went out and he bought some sheep. He sold those sheep and made a profit. He bought some camels and sold them for a profit. God blessed his wife. He would have had to bless his wife for them to have more kids. She had three daughters that were, the Bible says, the fairest of the fair. Their names were Cassie, Keren and Jemima, which means beautiful eyes.

The people were a blessing to the work of God because of the Covenant. In order for us to be a blessing, we, ourselves, must be blessed. We have a mission; our mission is to help the poor. With our blessing from God, we can accomplish our mission. We can spread the gospel, send our children to college, and live a fruitful life. God imparts blessings, and, by doing so, gives us power to release blessings into our world.

RUTH AND BOAZ

In the Book of Ruth, there is an interesting story.

> *"So Boaz took Ruth, and she was his wife: and when he went in unto her, the LORD gave her conception, and she bare a son. And the women said unto Naomi, Blessed be the LORD, which hath not left thee this day without a kinsman, that his name may be famous in Israel"*
> *--Ruth 4:13-14*

Ruth was the daughter-in-law of Naomi. They went to Moab to live because there was a famine in the land. But sickness came. Elimelech, Naomi's husband, passed away. Then her two sons died. Naomi went back to her homeland, and she and Ruth went on with their lives. Ruth decided to return with Naomi to Bethlehem. Ruth said, *"Your people shall be my people. Your God shall be my God."* They went away full, but they came back empty. They were impoverished.

The Law of Moses provided for the poor. When crops were planted, they did not harvest around the edges of the field for the sake of the poor. Ruth gleaned in the fields of Boaz.

The Bible says that Boaz was a wealthy man. By being wealthy not only pertained to money, but it also pertained to a good name. Boaz, whose name means swiftness, probably had been a warrior and an army hero. He had come back from the war a rich man. He was a legend in that part of the country. He owned land. Ruth worked in his fields. Boaz kept his eye on her, but evidently he was an older man, and referred to her as *"daughter."*

Naomi talked to Ruth, *"We have a law that says God will provide for the widow, especially if she has no children. God has ordained your nearest kin to marry you, and that is Boaz."*

One night she went to Boaz while he was asleep. In a non-sexual and non-sensuous way, she went and lay down at his feet. It evidently was a cold night. She put her feet under his blanket. When she touched his feet, he awoke.

"You are my kinsman redeemer. I have come to remind you of your obligation."

He said, *"You are more righteous than I am. But there is a more near-kin than I am. I will go and intercede with him tomorrow."*

Boaz and Ruth later married. The witnesses gathered and they pronounced a blessing on their marriage. All the people that were in the gate, and the elders said, *"We are witnesses. The Lord make the woman that has come into thine house, like Rachel and like Leah, which two did build the house of Israel; and do thou worthily; and be famous in Bethlehem; and let thy house be like the house of Perez, whom Tamar bear unto Judah the seed which the Lord shall give thee to this young woman." (Ruth 4:11-12)*

The elders of the city and friends gathered around and they blessed that couple. *"May you be famous. May you be blessed. May you have children. May they grow up to be mighty."* Their son became the grandfather of King David. David, of course, is the forefather of Jesus.

Every word that was spoken in that blessing came to pass.

In the Old Testament, the people blessed, and when a father was to die, he would line up his sons and his daughters, and he would pronounce a blessing upon them.

The "blessing" was one of the most valuable inheritance children could receive. God has commanded that we are to bless!

THE POWER TO BLESS

CHAPTER 4

THREE AREAS TO BLESS

"…the Lord hath blessed me for thy sake."
--Genesis 30:27

There are three areas in which we are to speak blessings to:

Conditions, Situations and Circumstances

Stop what you are doing and start blessing. Maybe you are not fulfilled at your job. Quit cursing your job. Start blessing it. Start blessing what you are doing. You are going to see things change and things happen in your life.

The Bible tells a story about twins, Jacob and Esau. Esau was his father's favorite. He received the birthright. Jacob traded Esau soup for his birthright---for the blessing of God upon his life. You remember the story in the Bible how Jacob deceived his own, blind father. In spite of that, his father said, *"Before I die, I am going to lay hands upon you and impart a blessing."* Giving a blessing to the next generation had prime importance in Bible days. I only wish it held that same value to fathers today.

When Isaac was ready to impart the blessing, he sent Esau to kill venison and make him "savory meat." But Rebekah spoke to Jacob,

"I heard your father speak unto Esau. Go now to the flock, and fetch me two goats. And I will make savory meat for your father."

--Genesis 27:6-9.

"Jacob put skins of goats on his hands and came to his father, 'I am Esau thy firstborn: I pray thee sit and eat of thy venison, that thy soul may bless me.' "
--Genesis 27:19.

Then Isaac blessed Jacob, *"God give thee the dew of heaven, and the fatness of the earth, and plenty of corn and wine. Let people serve thee, and nations bow down to thee. Cursed be everyone that curseth thee, and blessed be he that blesseth thee."*
-- Genesis 27:28-29.

Jacob had scarcely left when Esau returned from his hunt and came to his father. When he discovered Jacob had stolen his blessing he wept bitterly. Then Esau said to his father, "Do you have a blessing for me? Please bless me."

Isaac said, *"Behold thy dwelling shall be the fatness of the earth, and of the dew of heaven from above."*
--Genesis 27:39.

It is interesting how the descendants of Esau eventually settled in Saudi Arabia. They became the modern day Saudis. Their inheritance was the "fatness of the earth." If one takes fat and puts it in the skillet it becomes oil. The oil of Saudi Arabia was the blessing from Isaac.

Thank God for the power to bless.

Esau saw Jacob and said, *"I am going to kill you. You've stolen my blessing."* Jacob fled for his life. So he went to live with his uncle Laban. While there, he prospered. Laban had never been so blessed. Laban told Jacob, *"I have learned by experience (a divine, fortune teller) that the Lord hath blessed me for thy sake." Genesis 30:27.*

When the blessings of God come upon you, everybody that gets in contact with you is blessed. He was blessed and prosperous.

There are people who always try to blame other people for their problems. But Jacob went away empty, but he came back full.

BLESSINGS OVER PEOPLE

We are to pronounce blessings over our families, companions, and people with whom we work. We are not to curse people, we are to bless them. Seventy percent of the wealth of the world today is in the seed of Abraham. We are blessed today because of words that were spoken. A man has the power to bless or curse his family. Proverbs 25:28 *says, "He that hath no rule over his own spirit is like a city broken down, without walls."* In ancient days city walls protected people's lives. They kept back armies. If you do not have control over words spoken, the walls are broken down and Satan comes in and destroys you. Words of anger can destroy a marriage.

We are not in the cursing business. We are in the blessing business. We are to bless our enemies. We are to pray for them. When our enemies do not have food to eat, we are to give them food. It heaps coals of fire upon their head. If you keep your attitude right with God, He can bring a healing in your life. God has called us to bless, and not to curse. We are to bless circumstances and conditions and situations---to bless people.

BLESS GOD

"Bless the Lord, oh my soul, and all that is within me, bless his holy name. Bless the Lord, oh my soul, and forget not all of his benefits,who forgiveth all thine iniquities; who healeth all thy diseases."
--Psalms 103:1-3

Sometimes we take things for granted. We do not realize how blessed we really are. Maybe we go through some difficulties; and we get mad at God. *"I am mad at God because I am not blessed."* Well, maybe there is a reason why you are not blessed.

God has commanded us to bless the Lord. As the above scripture says, there are benefits when you begin to bless the Lord. There are benefits when you begin to praise God. Begin to praise and worship the Lord. Begin to hallow His Name. Father, we bless Your Name. The sacrifice of praise is the fruit of our lips, continuing to give praise unto Him. We bless Your Name.

I do not want to lose out, because I did not bless God. It would be sad to miss God's favor because I was not grateful. I want to have a blessing vocabulary. When I say *"God bless you"* I want to mean it. I want to release

God's blessings into your life.

Did you know the blessings of God are for the righteous?

If you are outside of salvation, you are outside of God's blessings. There is a door that opens up to the blessings of God---that is salvation through His son, Jesus Christ. Jesus is the only door. Good works will not save a person.

NOBEL PRIZE:
A PERSON WHO BLESSES PEOPLE

Alfred Nobel was reading the paper one day and was reading his own obituary. It said, *"An inventor of dynamite, died yesterday. He devised a way for more people to be killed in a war than ever before. And he died a very rich man."* Actually, it was his brother who died. But the paper had gotten the situation confused. So, he said I do not want to be known as a person who killed people. I want to be known as a person who blessed people. So he initiated the Nobel Peace Prize which gives awards to scientists and writers who foster peace, and not war.

THE POWER TO BLESS

CHAPTER 5

POWER OF THE TONGUE

"A word fitly spoken is like apples of gold in pictures of silver."
                                    --Proverbs 25:11

We have the power to bless!

In another translation it says, *"A word spoken in season is like apples of gold on trays of silver."* In the days in which this was written, a golden apple was significant with a great honor. If you were to achieve some great notoriety, and you got a reward, the king would present to you a golden apple. You would take that golden apple and you would set it upon your mantel. When people would come by, they would say, *"Oh, you've got a golden apple!"* It meant you were a person of honor. It meant that you had achieved something great.

The Bible says that a word that is fitly spoken or a word of blessing is one of the highest honors and gifts that God has given us. It is like a golden apple on a silver tray. The words that we speak and the blessing that we proclaim can work for us. The greatest blessing that you can give to people is to begin to bless them with the Word of God. Give them a scripture.

You have power to bless.

"He will bless them that fear the LORD, both small and great. The LORD shall increase you more and more, you and your children. Ye are blessed of the LORD which made heaven and earth. The heaven, even the heavens, are the LORD'S: but the earth hath he given to the children of men."

--Psalms 115:14-16

One night as I was preaching, I stopped in the middle of my sermon, and on the second row, there was a lady that was sitting with her two children. I said, *"I have a promise for you."* It was Psalm 115:14, *"The Lord shall increase you more and more, you and your children. You are blessed of the Lord..."*

When they went home that day, the little boy turned to his mother, *"Momma, that promise was for me."* You see, the father had divorced his mother that year. And the son had really blamed himself. His grades, which had been good grades before the divorce, went to D's and F's. He was failing. *"Momma, I believe God is going to increase me, more and more, every day. God is going to help me to do better."*

When the next report card came out, those D's and F's were C's. The next grading period, they came up to B's. Before the end of that year, they were back up to A's.

What happened?

A word fitly spoken is like apples of gold on trays of silver.

What are you going to do? Are you going to bless your family? Are you going to curse them? Are you going to fuss at your spouse? God is watching what YOU will say! There is great power in the tongue---YOUR tongue!

LIFE'S TURNING POINT

There was a fifth grade teacher named Miss Ballard. She had a student by the name of Teddy. She had only been teaching for two years. As a cardinal rule among teachers they should not have favorites. But everyone, from time to time, has one. The one thing they can never do, however, is have a student they dislike.

Teddy did not dress well. He did not keep himself clean. He was a slow learner. He was behind the entire class. Miss Ballard just did not like this boy. He was not discourteous, but he was just not on the same level as the other students. When she graded his paper, the cross marks were always a little larger and a little redder than necessary. She would write remarks like "poor work" "attitude is not good."

Just before the Christmas holidays came, she was going over the grades and she knew that Teddy could not pass. So she pulled out his cumulative folder that went all the way back to the first grade. She began to examine these and he had low grades for four years. In the first grade the teacher had written, "He has a positive attitude and works hard, but has a very poor home situation." The second grade teacher wrote, "Mother is terribly ill. No help at home." The third grade teacher wrote, "Pleasant boy, but too serious." The fourth grade teacher wrote, "Slow learner. This year his mother passed away. The father shows no interest at all."

Yet, all of these teachers had passed him. Miss Ballard said, "Well, they all did not do their job. They all should have failed him. I guess I am the only one who has the nerve to do what needs to be done in Teddy's life."

But during the Christmas party that the class had, each of the students brought their teacher a gift. Patiently, she would open each gift and comment. Then she came to Teddy's gift. It was in a brown paper sack. It had a string wrapped around it. Written on the sack in pencil was, *"To Miss Ballard. Merry Christmas. From Teddy."* When she opened the sack in front of the students, she pulled out a half bottle of cheap cologne. Then there was a bracelet with a few cheap stones missing.

She dabbed the cologne on her ear and said, "Oh, it smells so good." She put it on some of the other girls to try to make Teddy feel good. Then she put the bracelet on her arm and said, "Isn't this such a beautiful bracelet."

Then as the class was leaving that day, Teddy remained at his seat, and he was the last one to go. As he came to Miss Ballard, he said, "I sure am glad you like that cologne. You smell just like my mother. That was her cologne. Her bracelet looks so pretty on you. Merry Christmas. I love you."

After he left, Miss Ballard placed her head on her desk. She cried and she sobbed. She said, "God, forgive me, I have not shown love towards this child. Lord, help me to help him."

When the Christmas holidays were over, Teddy came back to school. She took him aside and said, "Teddy, I am going to help you pass the fifth grade. You are going to stay after school and I am going to work with you. I am going to tutor you, and you are going to learn this work." That is exactly what she did. She worked with him, and his grades rose and he began to learn. He passed the fifth grade.

The years passed. Miss Ballard had always wondered what happened to little Teddy. Then, seven years later, a letter came: "Dear Miss Ballard, I graduated second in my class from high school. As I look back, you were the turning point in my life. Thank you so much."

Then four years later, she received another letter: "Dear Miss Ballard, next week I am graduating valedictorian of the university. It has not been easy. But I finally made it. Thanks again for all the kindnesses you showed me. It really changed my life."

She received a third letter four years later: "Dear Miss Ballard, as of today I am Theodore Stollard M.D. How about that? I made it through medical school. Also I am getting married on July 27th. If you could come and sit where mom would have been seated, it would really mean a lot. My father died last year and I have no family left. Sincerely, Dr. Theodore Stollard."

She immediately wrote a letter of congratulations, "I will be glad to see you at the wedding. I look forward to it. Sincerely, Miss Ballard."

THE POWER TO BLESS

CHAPTER 6

SPEAK AND RELEASE THE BLESSINGS

"But the word is very nigh unto thee, in thy mouth, and in thy heart, that thou mayest do it."
--Deuteronomy 30:14

In a time when people operate in fear, there shall be a marked difference between God's people and the world's people. There shall be a clear mark upon believers and upon their families. As Believers, we are to live and to multiply, and possess the promises of God.

We must learn how to proclaim the blessings of God for our life. We must have the blessings of God. The blessings of God make all the difference. It starts with you SPEAKING and RELEASING the power of God in your life, through BLESSING OTHERS!

"The righteous shall flourish like the palm tree: he shall grow like a cedar in Lebanon."
--Psalms 92:12

In this scripture, there is a palm tree is in the middle of a desert where nothing can grow and where nothing can sustain life. God says, *"My people shall flourish when nobody else flourishes. When there is not enough money to buy bread, my people shall sell the bread."* The *"cedars of Lebanon"* denotes durability.

That is what they use to build the palaces of kings. God's people shall be mighty. God's people shall be in places of authority. They shall endure.

God's people shall be blessed in the time of famine. Why? Because we know how to be blessed. We know how to bless our families. We know how to bless our children.

HOW TO BEGIN TO RELEASE BLESSINGS

This is something that everyone needs to know.... how to release blessings. That is the purpose of this book.

"For this commandment which I command thee this day, it is not hidden from thee, neither is it far off. It is not in heaven, that thou shouldest say, Who shall go up for us to heaven, and bring it unto us, that we may hear it, and do it? Neither is it beyond the sea, that thou shouldest say, Who shall go over the sea for us, and bring it unto us, that we may hear it, and do it? But the word is very nigh unto thee, in thy mouth, and in thy heart, that thou mayest do it."

--Deuteronomy 30:11-14

There are a series of messages preached by Moses in Deuteronomy 28, he talks about the blessings and curses. Then he says, *"For this commandment."* TO BE BLESSED---IT'S A COMMANDMENT! If we are not blessed, we cannot multiply. We cannot defeat our enemies. We cannot accomplish what God wants us to accomplish. He commanded us to be blessed.

THE BLESSING MUST COME
OUT OF YOUR MOUTH

The first principle on how to release the blessing is *to SPEAK THE BLESSING.* The Word of God gets into your heart, then it gets into your mouth as you speak it and release it in the Name of the Lord.

No matter how poor I was, I spoke BLESSINGS!

I first began pastoring in Lexington, Kentucky. It was a troubled church. After three months I had a "back door" revival. More people went out the back door than came in the front door of the church. We "grew" from 40 people to 20 people.

After that, I knew I had to stay at that small church. They didn't pay very much at all. Literally, to survive, I had to visit church members about suppertime. If it hadn't been for that (I was single at the time) I would have gone through many hungry weeks. This is how I learned to fast. Finally, the church began to grow and we began to have a move of God.

I got up to where I was making $75 a week. Then I got married. Sometimes I didn't get paid. We were trying to survive. I cannot express to you how difficult it was.

One winter, I could not pay the gas payment on our house. My in-laws came up to see me. There was an evangelist who came up from Key West, Florida. They were not used to the cold winter. You could sit and see daylight through the walls of my house.

When I arrived home, Margaret came and said,

"Bob, they have cut the gas off. My folks just got here. The evangelist is staying here. His wife has been wrapped up in a blanket. She is having chills." It was a terrible situation.

I was so discouraged. While praying, and reading the Bible, I read Deuteronomy 30:14, *"But the word is very nigh unto thee, and in thy heart to do it."*

I began to proclaim, God is beginning to work a financial miracle in my life. I prayed this for over an hour. After an hour, the Lord spoke to me. He said, *"Son, what would you do if you were the son of a king, and you had all the money you wanted?"*

"Lord, what I would do is to pay off these bills." The Lord said, *"No, you would not do that. That would not be a worry in your life."*

If you had all the money in the world, would you be worried about your car payment? Would you be worried about your light bill? No.

I said, *"Lord, I have always wanted to own property. I would buy some property."* God said, *"Go buy your property."* I told Margaret, *"God is blessing us. I am going to buy some property."*

Remember, they are cutting our lights off. The gas was already cut off. I could not remember the last time I took my wife out to eat. So I called the real estate agent. I said, *"I am looking for some rental property."* This lady came and sold us some apartments on Limestone Street in Lexington, Kentucky. She showed me a duplex and a triplex. She told me the price on it and declared, *"This is a real good bargain for you."*

Suddenly, I felt a long, "yellow streak" go down my back. I thought, *"What am I doing here? I do not have any money. Why am I doing this?"* So, in trying to get out of a bad situation, I said, *"Well, I am really not interested in just these two pieces of property, if I could buy the whole block, I would be interested."*

Her reply, *"I didn't know you were that big of an operator?"* Later that day, she called me and said, *"The doctor that owns these two pieces of property, he owns the whole block. He is willing to sell it all to you."* How much? When she told me how much, I replied, *"That is too much!"*

"How much are you willing to offer?" I am thinking, *"Oh God, please deliver me."* I said, *"Well, I would not want to insult him, the price is quite a bit lower. She said, "Go ahead, and just make the offer."* I did, and he accepted it!

To be quite honest with you, this was a big mistake. I was just testing the Word of God. In my moment of weakness, I was trying to step out in faith. Now I was out where I did not feel the presence of the Lord. I was trying to put it into action. It was scary. It came to the time of closing and I had not been able to raise any money. Nobody would loan me any money. I told them, *"I am sorry. I am not able to close on this deal. I could not get the financing."* The doctor blew up and threatened to sue me.

Then he cooled down and said, *"I will loan you the money. I will carry the financing."* He sold me all that property. I knew I had a hold of something. I knew this "faith thing" really worked. I know you can speak to mountains. I know you can begin to proclaim the blessings of God. It really works.

1.   YOU MUST BEGIN TO SPEAK GOD'S PROMISES.

2.   DO NOT SPEAK THINGS THAT OUGHT NOT TO BE SPOKEN.

> *"Out of the same mouth proceedeth blessing and cursing. My brethren, these things ought not so to be. Doth a fountain send forth at the same place sweet water and bitter?"*
> ---*James 3:10-11*

Do not allow your tongue to sin by talking negative things. *"I am going under. We do not have any money. We are broke. I don't know how we are going to make it next month."*

You have got to choose what is going to be your future. You have got to proclaim it. You've got to speak it. You have got to proclaim it when there is no help in sight. You have got to speak your blessings, **<u>NO MATTER WHAT YOUR CIRCUMSTANCE IS.</u>**

You have a choice. You can't speak both faith and doubt and expect faith results. Choose faith words.

> *"I am prosperous. I am overcoming.*
> *I am more than a conqueror.*
> *I've got more than enough.*
> *God has opened the windows of heaven and He is pouring out blessings upon me.*
> *I am blessed in the Name of Jesus."*

You cannot go around speaking blessings; then go around speaking curses. "Sweet and bitter water does not come out of the same fountain." A person of faith does not go around belly-aching and crying the blues and telling everyone how bad it is. Shake it off. Stand up like a man. Proclaim the blessings of God in your life.

> *"Not rendering evil for evil, or railing for railing: but contrariwise blessing; knowing that ye are thereunto called, that ye should inherit a blessing. For he that will love life, and see good days, let him refrain his tongue from evil, and his lips that they speak no guile:"*
> *--I Peter 3:9-10*

Peter wrote this to the Church. The Church was scattered at that time through all of Asia Minor and Rome. Do not speak evil. If you want to be blessed, start speaking righteous words. Start blessing, instead of cursing. Do not criticize. Do not talk evil of people. Do not gossip about people.

God blesses YOU, so you can be a blessing.

Once I had my cousin to come over to my house. My cousin pastors a small church in Lebanon Junction, Kentucky. He has been very faithful. He has had to work another job to make ends meet, because much of the time the church has not been able to pay him. When I look at pastors like that, I think to myself, *"They are the real heroes."* I pastor a church that is able to give me a nice salary. But there are many great men of God who go into parts of the vineyard that requires them to work on the side.

As he was getting ready to leave, I said, *"I've got*

something for you." I went upstairs. I got two suits out of the closet, as well as some ties and shirts. I told him, "*I want to give you these suits.*"

"*Bob, you will never believe what happened to me this week. I had a blowout on Sunday morning. I had to get out and climb underneath my truck to get the tire out. I ruined my suit. I have been praying that God would help me to get another suit.*"

You see, God blesses us, because He wants us to be a blessing.

HOW TO RELEASE GOD'S BLESSINGS

John 11 tells the story of Lazarus. Lazarus was a dear family friend of Jesus. They ministered unto him and they let him stay in their home. Bethany was about six miles from Jerusalem. When he would come to Jerusalem, He often would stay with Lazarus. Lazarus died. Jesus finally came.

"*Then they took away the stone from the place where the dead was laid. And Jesus lifted up his eyes, and said, Father, I thank thee that thou hast heard me. And I knew that thou hearest me always: but because of the people which stand by I said it, that they may believe that thou hast sent me. And when he thus had spoken, he cried with a loud voice, Lazarus, come forth. And he that was dead came forth, bound hand and foot with graveclothes: and his face was bound about with a napkin. Jesus saith unto them, Loose him, and let him go.*"

--John 11:41-44

It was not God's will that Lazarus was dead. Sometimes blessings die. Lazarus was a blessing unto Christ, but he was dead. Jesus came to resurrect the blessing back to him. What did He do to resurrect that blessing?

The first thing He did was to roll away the stone.

Jesus lifted up his eyes and said, *"Father, I thank thee, that thou hearest Me..."*

You've got to be filled with faith. *"Lord, you always hear me. I knew that thou hearest me always."*

Let me tell you, God always hears us! When you have that attitude, and you begin to recognize that your prayers are being heard of God regardless of how you feel, that takes faith. It is a higher level of faith.

I am so sick and tired of being around people that when they feel good, God has heard them. When they do not feel good, God has deserted them.

Come on! Shake it off! Stand up like a man and start proclaiming what God has in store for you. God is not a God just of your feelings. The thermometer of what God is doing cannot be your feelings. Sometimes you do not feel good. As a pastor, there are times I do not feel like preaching. There are times I do not even feel saved. But what difference does it make? I am saved by the blood of Jesus. I preach because God has called me to preach. I do not preach because the weather is 72 degrees. Or because it is hot or because it is cold. I serve God because He has called me to serve Him! I do it in faith, in the Name of Jesus!

Jesus lifts up His voice and says, *"Father, I thank you that you always hear my prayer."*

In your heart, even as you read this book, proclaim, *"God always hears my prayer. Father I thank you, because you always hear me when I pray."*

Then he spoke the words, *"Lazarus, come forth!"*

How did He get Lazarus to come forth? He spoke it! He imparted life. There was an impartation of life and blessing when He spoke the words.

You see, the blessings are there for us!

They are in the Bible. God spoke these promises and these promises are within the Word of God.

Lazarus was there and there were stones upon him. He has to be resurrected by faith. There has to be an impartation. The impartation to the blessings that God has promised in His Word is when you stand and you proclaim it in faith. YOU must speak and proclaim the blessings of God for you!

"Lazarus, come forth!"

"Money, come forth!"

"Healing, come forth!"

Speak the blessing!

THE POWER TO BLESS

CHAPTER 7

BLESS YOUR FAMILY

"...I will bless them."
--Numbers 6:27

"Pastor, I do not know how to give a blessing. I do not know how to release these blessings to people." Here is how to release the blessings of God in your family.

"And the LORD spake unto Moses, saying, Speak unto Aaron and unto his sons, saying, On this wise ye shall bless the children of Israel, saying unto them, The LORD bless thee, and keep thee: The LORD make his face shine upon thee, and be gracious unto thee: The LORD lift up his countenance upon thee, and give thee peace. And they shall put my name upon the children of Israel; and I will bless them."
--Numbers 6:22-27

KNOW YOU HAVE THE AUTHORITY TO BLESS! In the Name of the Lord.

In the Bible, the Covenant was with Abraham, Isaac and Jacob. Rebekkah was married to Isaac. This meant she was just as much in covenant relationship as Isaac was. God chose her. The blessing was placed upon her and God fulfilled that blessing. We have the right to give blessings to our sisters and brothers and our siblings, our family.

"The sceptre shall not depart from Judah, nor a lawgiver from between his feet, until Shiloh come; and unto him shall the gathering of the people be."

--Genesis 49:10

It was time for Jacob to die, so he began to impart a word of blessing. He lined up his sons and began to prophesy to them, *"Judah, the hand of God is upon you. Out of you shall come the Messiah, the one that shall bruise the head of the serpent. Dan shall judge his people as one of the tribes of Israel."(Genesis 49)*

Do you know who came out of the tribe of Dan? Samson.

OUR RIGHT TO BLESS OUR CHILDREN

Not only do we have the right and authority to bless our brothers and our sisters, we have the right to bless our children. That is our God-given right and God-given authority.

The day before my father died, he was in great health. We had lunch together.

He said, *"Son, I want to tell you something. God has ordained you to be the pastor to succeed me. I have built this church. But you are going to have to pay for it. (We laughed). But the day will come when God will send a great revival and you will build the new church. You always remember that. If anything happens to me, I want you to watch certain situations. There is a group of people that have caused me a great trouble. You deal with that in wisdom. Watch this person. God is going to help you. And you are going to do well."*

The next morning, my father died. As I began to ponder on the words that he spoke to me, they really were prophetic words. He did not know it at the time. I did not know it at the time. But my father had spoken wisdom over my life.

The group that had risen up was a group of people that had a church on our property. They had become very carnal. My dad had tried to work with them. In the process of trying to counsel with the two factions in that church, they got into a fist fight in my dad's living room. To have peace, my dad allowed this group that was using the church, to have two churches. There were both using our building. I prayed, and God showed me how to handle it. God brought peace. And I dealt with each of these issues as they came. But it was prophetic.

But Dad had already pronounced a blessing upon me. You can do the same, for your son or your daughter!

When we began to ponder about the moving of our church, I fasted for 40 days and I walked the city. While walking, God reminded me of those words that had been spoken through my father, "The day will come when you will build the big church." It seemed like it was a confirmation that we were headed in the right direction.

I admonish you to always stay in close communication with your children. No matter how rebellious they may become, BLESS THEM!

"And they brought young children to him, that he should touch them: and his disciples

rebuked those that brought them. But when Jesus saw it, he was much displeased, and said unto them, Suffer the little children to come unto me, and forbid them not: for of such is the kingdom of God. Verily I say unto you, Whosoever shall not receive the kingdom of God as a little child, he shall not enter therein. And he took them up in his arms, put his hands upon them, and blessed them."

--Mark 10:13-16

I wish I could have been there, in Mark 10. I wish I could have brought my children. I wonder what happened to the children that He took into His arms that day and blessed? I wonder what words He said to them? I know the words of blessing changed the lives of those children.

I speak a blessing over my family. My family shall be blessed. My daughters shall marry righteous men. They will be full of faith and full of the Holy Ghost. My son shall marry a godly girl. They will prosper and be successful. My children shall not divorce. They shall be blessed and they shall succeed in the Name of Jesus Christ!

FORGIVENESS IS A PART OF BLESSINGS

I have a friend by the name of Roy who was always rejected by his father. His dad would make comments while he was in school, "Why can't you be like your brother?" He resented his father. He resented his brother.

He began to rebel. He grew his hair long. He got into the pharmaceutical business. He sold drugs. But later he got saved and married a godly girl. God called him to preach.

One morning while he was praying God spoke to him, "Do you love your father?"

"I respect my father. I honor my father, but no Lord, I don't really love him."

The Lord spoke to him to begin to love his father. And to go tell his father that he loved him. He battled with this for weeks. Then one evening as he sat down to eat supper, he told his wife, "I can't take this anymore, I've got to go see my father." He drove over to where his folks lived.

He went over to his dad and said, "Dad, I just want to tell you that I love you!" And then he left.

Every Saturday he began to go to see his parents. He would just see if there was anything that needed to be done. He would cut the grass and help around the house. Every time he would leave he would tell his dad that he loved him. Then one Saturday as he got ready to leave he went over to his father and put his arms around him and kissed him.

His dad said, "Don't be getting mushy on me."

As he was praying one day, the Lord spoke to him to write a letter to his father and tell him how much he appreciated him. Roy wrote, "Dear Dad, I just wanted to take a moment to tell you how much I appreciate you. You always made sure that we went to school, had nice clothes to wear. You worked hard to provide shelter and food. I will never forget this. Thank you very much. I love you. Your son, Roy."

A couple of weeks passed and one day he asked his mother, "Did Dad ever receive a letter from me?"

"Well he sure did."

"He has never told me about it."

"No, but he has told everybody else about it. He keeps the letter in his back pocket. He shows it to everybody that comes to the house."

Roy and his father became the best of friends. One Saturday when Roy was unable to come over, his dad said to his wife, "What's wrong with Roy. Maybe we ought to check on him. Maybe he is sick. Maybe there is a problem. Maybe he had an accident."

One day his dad said, "Roy, I have always worked hard. I've never been a church-going man, but always wanted to do good."

Finally Roy said, "Dad, are you saying you want to become a Christian?"

"Yes, that is what I am trying to say."

Roy led his father to the Lord. Then, a few weeks later, he baptized him in water at the church. Every time the door was open, his dad would be there at church. Two months passed, and his father was diagnosed with cancer. One month later he died. Roy buried his own father.

THE POWER OF BLESSING

CHAPTER 8

CURSES ARE "BLESSING BLOCKERS"

> *"If ye will not hear, and if ye will not lay it to heart, to give glory unto my name, saith the LORD of hosts, I will even send a curse upon you, and I will curse your blessings: yea, I have cursed them already, because ye do not lay it to heart."*
> *--Malachi 2:2*

As we have already read, Paul says, *"I want you to bless, and curse not."* For him to warn them not to curse, must have meant there was power to curse. Cursing can do as much in the negative as blessings can do in the positive.

I think we have all seen that in churches. People get bitter towards others and they begin to get on gossiping campaigns, and telephone brigades. They get mad at the preacher. They start criticizing the preacher. Pretty soon, the church is splintered and the church is destroyed.

People are destroyed by planting curses.

You can start criticizing your wife, until your wife finally says, *"I've had it. I can't do anything to please that man. I am going to go ahead and not improve my looks. I am going to do what I want, and he can do whatever he wants."* Pretty soon, they fall out of love. That is how divorce creeps in.

When the husband says, *"I am sick and tired of this nagging wife."* Do you know what it is? It is pronouncing curses. You may not call it that. But that is what it is.

You pronounce a curse on your children, *"Oh, you're never going to do anything. You are lazy. You are not going to succeed. You are stupid."* Pretty soon, they are going to begin to believe that. In their fragile makeup, they rationalize, *"I cannot improve. I cannot be successful. Maybe I am dumb. Maybe I am doomed to live a life of defeat."*

I do not know anybody who gets any meaner than carnal Christians. You get Christians stirred up, they can be just as mean as a rattlesnake. A few years ago, some people got mad at me and actually said, *"Yes, you are going to have a member of your family die."* Can you imagine people wanting a member of your family to die?

That week, I was on a four-wheeler with my son. I said, *"All right, Justin, you drive it."*

"I don't know how to drive it, Daddy."

"Just drive it the way you've seen me."

So he floor-boarded it. Then he made a sharp turn. When he did, it flipped over. It threw me off. The four-wheeler went upside down. I saw Justin upside down, still holding on to it. I quickly prayed, *"Oh God, spare his life, don't let that curse of death come upon him."* He let go and fell. That four-wheeler fell right beside him and bounced; he was unhurt.

But the enemy, your critics, would say, *"That was a*

judgment of God." Your friends would have said, *"Oh, the devil tried to kill him."* It's either God's judgment or the devil, depending upon whose side you are on. Do not be a part of that kind of talk or thought process. It is a curse. You become guilty of spiritual witchcraft.

Shake yourself free from that stuff. Do not let that be in your spirit. Yes, there are people who come against God's anointed. There are people that come against you. But that does not give you the right to put a curse on them. That does not give you the right to prophesy death and destruction and poverty.

The Bible says we are to bless those who curse us. We are to do good for those who despitefully use us. And if they go broke, we are to give them food, money, and help pay their light bill so they can make it on in life.

When you do that, it heaps coals of fire upon their head.

Oh, this Christian life, it can be tough. Sometimes you want to pray, *"Lord, blast them."* But God says, *"Bless them!"* Paul wrote and said, *"Bless, and curse not,"* because there is a power to curse. Oh, thank God, the blessing is much stronger than the cursing!

The cursing business, pronouncing judgment and proclaiming evil upon others is straight from the very pit of hell. Curses are of the devil. Blessings are from God!

"WHAT GOES AROUND, COMES AROUND"

Who do you think you are anyway? Jesus was God;

and He turned the other cheek. They beat Him, and He spoke no defense. They do not build monuments to critics. They build monuments to people who love and people who accomplish great things for the Lord.

If you start cursing people, it will come back on you. Sooner or later, God's presence will lift from your life. Each day bless your family, even before they leave for school, then God will release angels to help fulfill your words.

> *"Bless the LORD, ye his angels, that excel in strength, that do his commandments, hearkening unto the voice of his word."*
> *--Psalm 103:20*

When we speak blessings, angels help accomplish those words that are spoken.

But when you start cursing people, that same angel that fought for you, will turn and eventually fight against you. How does judgment come to people that attack the righteous? Believe me, God knows how to take care of those people. God knows how to spank those people. Let God bring His own judgment.

But we are called to bless and not to curse.

You start criticizing people, talking nasty to your spouse, criticizing the work of God and pronouncing curses, it will not be long before you are cold in your relationship with God.

You will go for weeks and months and you will not hear God's voice. You will not sense God's presence.

Why? God has moved His presence out of your camp. He has moved away from you.

It is a dangerous thing to get into the cursing business. I want to be a blesser, to release blessings upon people.

THE CURSE OF A LIQUOR STORE

Years ago, Margaret and I pastored in Lexington. Next door to our church was a liquor store. It just grieved me to see that liquor store next to the church. I would go by and say, *"I rebuke you in the Name of Jesus. I curse this nasty place."* The lady that worked there had two children. Her parents owned the store. She put her children in our day care. I was so spiritually naïve, I wanted to curse those people, but God wanted to bless them. She brought her children to our day care. They got saved!

They decided to get baptized in water. The mother and the grandmother and their husbands (who owned it), came to the church to watch their children get baptized. And they got saved!

The daughter said, *"Oh, we've got to reach the world and all these people that come into our liquor store, praise God we are going to witness for Jesus."*

She bought Bibles to sell in the liquor store. People would come in and as they would check out with their Jack Daniels and there was a Bible for sale. One of the liquor salesman came in, who was a back-slidden preacher. He said, *"My God, why have you got Bibles in this liquor store? This hurts our business."* She began to talk to him about how she got saved. He started reading the Bible. He said, *"Where do you go to church?"*

"We go right here." He came the next Sunday. He brought his wife and they got saved. They brought their children; they got saved. His son became a deacon in the church.

It's the power of speaking. I was speaking curses that the building would burn down. But God wanted to save those families! Eventually, the liquor store went out of business, but not before the families got saved!

We are to bless and not to curse.

THINGS THAT BLOCK BLESSINGS

Sometimes there are things that hold back the blessings of God. Let me tell you what the Bible says some of those things are.

"For ye know how that afterward, when he would have inherited the blessing, he was rejected: for he found no place of repentance, though he sought it carefully with tears."
--Hebrews 12:17

1. You do not treat your wife right. Or you do not treat your husband right. Did you know that could hinder your prayers?

2. There is sin in your life, maybe hidden sin. You cannot have hidden sin in your life and expect God to bless you. If you do, then God puts His stamp of

approval on that unforgiveness, or on that lust, or that hidden sin that you have.

3. Doubt, unbelief and prayerlessness. Did you know that prayerlessness is a sin? It was Samuel who said, *"I will not sin unto God by ceasing to pray for you."* You have got to remove the stone. You have got to ask God for cleansing. God needs to fill you with faith. As you bless--and not curse-- God will fill you with the power of His Word.

THE POWER TO BLESS

CONCLUSION

PRAYER OF BLESSING

There is power to bless in our words. God has called me to bless you. I will not curse you. I will not speak evil of you. But I will bless you and your families in the Name of Jesus.

I am praying the following blessings for you and your family. Begin to pray and speak these blessings for YOU! Believe with me as I pray…

I WILL

…have children who will want to learn; and will be the smartest children in their class.

…go to work early and leave after everybody leaves.

…work harder than anybody on your job at your business.

…not be lazy, but God will bless me.

…find favor with my employer.

…advance and prosper.

…be wealthy.

…succeed in the Name of Jesus, even when others fail.

…not be cursed with prejudice against whites or against blacks.

…be color blind in the Name of Jesus.

…be filled with the love of God.

…bless people that I work with.

…bless my employer.

…shake the hand of my boss and say, "I just want to bless you. We have been praying that this business will prosper. If there is anything extra you need me to do, you can count on me. I bless you in the Name of Jesus."

…have a correct attitude.

…be filled with joy and compassion.

…give to people that are hurting, as well as bless them.

…change the lives of people that I cross.

…receive from God as He open the windows of heaven upon me.

…see my children grow up to be mighty and when they are asked the question, "How did you succeed?" They will say it was my righteous grandparents that blessed me and were people of God and people of faith," in Jesus' Name.

…leave an inheritance to my children's children, in the Name of Jesus.

…be the salt of the earth, the light to the world, in Jesus' Name.

…hear His voice, as God speaks to me.

…receive prophetic utterances from my God.

…see things in the future that the world's crowd could never see because they are blinded through sin.

…be pure and righteous.

…be a soul winner.

My Friend, In the Name of Jesus, I bless you for the glory of God!

**"AS FOR ME AND MY HOUSE,
WE WILL SERVE THE LORD!"**

If this book has been a blessing to you,
feel free to contact us at:

**Bob Rodgers Ministries
P.O. Box 19229
Louisville, KY 40259
www.worldprayercenter.org
www.PrayerRadio.net**

Fasting & Prayer Books

By Bob Rodgers

Bob Rodgers
World Prayer Force
P.O. Box 19229
Louisville, Kentucky 40259
(502) 964-3304 EXT. 133

Books:

101 Reasons to Fast	$ 8.00
21 Days of Fasting	$10.00
Patterns of Prayer	$ 6.00
How to Pray the Lord's Prayer	$10.00
Miracle Book	$12.00
How Col. Sanders Found His Wealth	$ 2.00
How to Get Out of Debt in 50 Days	$10.00
5 Reasons Why People Do Not Fast	$ 6.00

PRODUCT ORDER FORM

Name: _____

Address: _____

City: _____ State: _____ Zip: _____

Phone: _____ E-Mail: _____

Amount of Purchase	**Method of Payment**
	Check ____ Cash ____
Sub Total ____	Credit Card: AmEx ____
Tax ____	Discover __ MC __ Visa __
Grand Total ____	KY Residents Add 6% Tax

Card No. & Exp. Date _____

Card Holder's Name (Please Print) _____

Card Holder's Signature _____